3,14

VEDIC MATHS

123

5 + 1 = 6

2×2=4

WORKBOOK 1

Om
KIDZ
An imprint of Om Books International

PREFACE

Vedic Mathematics is an ancient system of Mathematics. It was rediscovered from the Vedas by Swami Bharati Krishna Tirtha between 1911 and 1918. Vedic Mathematics is based on 16 sutras or word formulae. By using these formulae, the mind can be trained to solve mathematical problems with greater ease and accuracy.

Vedic Mathematics helps making mental calculations easier. It is a flexible system wherein the students have the liberty of inventing their own methods of calculations. This results in the calculations becoming much faster than regular methods. This enhances the students' interest in Mathematics.

The **Om Vedic Maths Workbook series** (Level 1 to Level 4) focuses on basic mathematical concepts such as addition, subtraction, multiplication and division that are explained in a fun and easy-to-understand manner. These books will cover the following sutras:

Digital root: Navashesh

All from 9 and the last from 10: Nikhilam

Vertically and cross-wise: Urdhva-Tiryagbhyam

One less than the previous one: Ekanyunena Purvena

The remainder by the last digit: Sheshanyankena Charamena

One more than previous one: Ekadhikena Purvena

Transpose and adjust: Paravartya Yojayet

The concepts of Vedic Mathematics are easy to understand, apply and remember. This book aims at developing an interest in Mathematics and making the subject easy and fun. It also aims at sharpening the student's mind and increase accuracy as well. This in turn will increase the student's concentration and logical thinking.

NAVASHESH

Numbers are made up of digits. For example: the digits of number 25 are 2 and 5. The digits of number 893 are 8, 9 and 3. When the digits of a number are added, the sum is the **Navashesh** or **digital root** of that number.

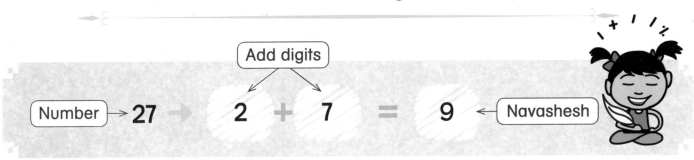

Add digits

Number → **27** → **2** + **7** = **9** ← Navashesh

Find the digital root of the following numbers.

1 15 → ☐ + ☐ = ☐

2 31 → ☐ + ☐ = ☐

3 521 → ☐ + ☐ + ☐ = ☐

4 124 → ☐ + ☐ + ☐ = ☐

5 404 → ☐ + ☐ + ☐ = ☐

6 701 → ☐ + ☐ + ☐ = ☐

NAVASHESH FOR LARGER NUMBERS

The Navashesh or digital root is always a **single-digit number**. Sometimes, when the digits of a number are added, the sum may be a two-digit number. In such cases, repeat the process until you arrive at a single-digit number.

| Number | Add digits | | Sum is a two-digit number | Add digits again | Navashesh |

$$245 \rightarrow 2 + 4 + 5 = 11 \rightarrow 1 + 1 = 2$$

Find the digital root of the following numbers.

1. 567 ➜ _____ = ◯ ➜ _____ = ◯

2. 639 ➜ _____ = ◯ ➜ _____ = ◯

3. 3459 ➜ _____ = ◯ ➜ _____ = ◯

4. 7690 ➜ _____ = ◯ ➜ _____ = ◯

5. 6898 ➜ _____ = ◯ ➜ _____ = ◯

NIKHILAM

Subtract the last digit of a number from 10. Subtract each of the remaining digits from 9. Put those numbers together and you will get the **Nikhilam** or **complement** of that number.

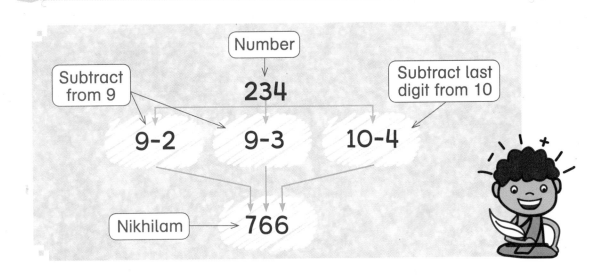

Find the Nikhilam or complement of the following numbers.

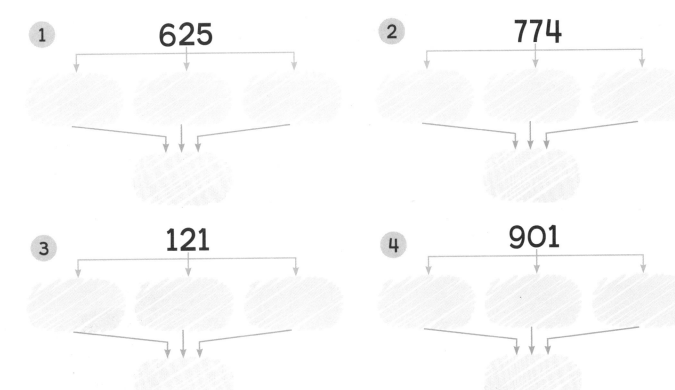

1. 625

2. 774

3. 121

4. 901

5 428

6 132

7 1235

8 1681

9 6708

Is the sum of the three-digit number and its Nikhilam 1000? Is the sum of the four-digit number and its Nikhilam 10,000? If it is, your answer is correct!

10 5471

6

DROP 10 METHOD

It is sometimes difficult to add three or more numbers. If you follow the **drop 10 method**, you can make addition simpler! The key is to never count above 10. When the running total becomes more than 10, stop, put a "−" or "." to represent 10 and use the remaining digits.

```
35      Start counting the ones.
14          Here, the sum is more than 10,
15 -         so add "−" to represent 10.
+ 41      5 + 4 = 9 + 5 = 14
         Continue by using only 4.
  5      - 4 + 1 = 5
```

Write 5 here. Carry 1 over to the tens − because "−" represents 10, 1 gets carried on the next digit.

```
35      Now, start counting the tens.
14          The carry over
15 -     3 + 1 = 4 + 1 = 5 + 4 = 9 + 1 = 10
+ 41
105     Write 10 before 5.
```

So, $35 + 14 + 15 + 41 = 105$

Add the following numbers using the drop 10 method.

1)
```
   16
   23
   22
 + 54
```

2)
```
   12
   27
   33
 + 36
```

3)
```
   15
   27
   36
 + 34
```

4)
```
   67
   11
   18
 + 20
```

5)
```
   84
   21
   65
 + 76
```

6)
```
   43
   27
   31
 + 42
```

7)
```
   23
   65
   33
   89
 + 40
```

8)
```
   11
   34
   12
   78
 + 98
```

9)
```
   45
   98
   56
   43
 + 12
```

The **drop 10 method** can be used with larger numbers as well. Using the same technique, carry the sum over to the tens and then the hundreds.

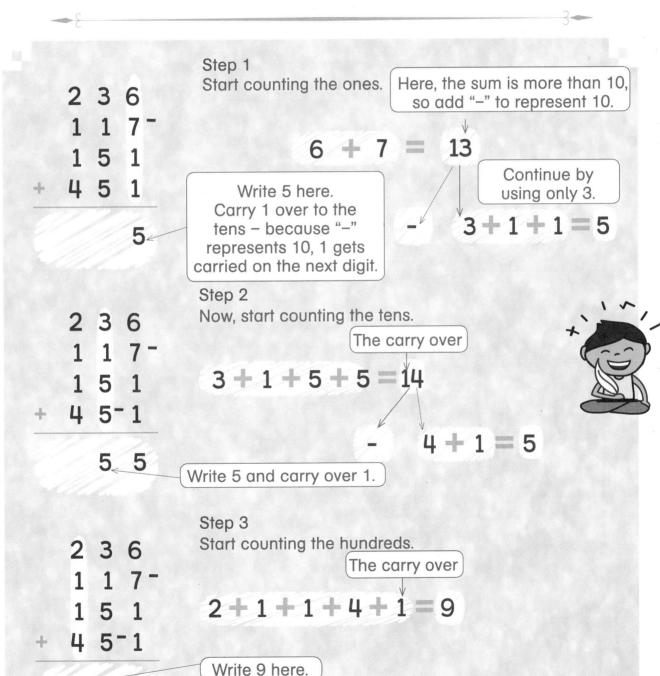

Step 1
Start counting the ones.

```
  2 3 6
  1 1 7⁻
  1 5 1
+ 4 5 1
  ─────
      5
```

Here, the sum is more than 10, so add "−" to represent 10.

$$6 + 7 = 13$$

Write 5 here. Carry 1 over to the tens − because "−" represents 10, 1 gets carried on the next digit.

Continue by using only 3.

$$- \quad 3 + 1 + 1 = 5$$

Step 2
Now, start counting the tens.

```
  2 3 6
  1 1 7⁻
  1 5 1
+ 4 5⁻1
  ─────
    5 5
```

The carry over

$$3 + 1 + 5 + 5 = 14$$

$$- \quad 4 + 1 = 5$$

Write 5 and carry over 1.

Step 3
Start counting the hundreds.

```
  2 3 6
  1 1 7⁻
  1 5 1
+ 4 5⁻1
  ─────
  9 5 5
```

The carry over

$$2 + 1 + 1 + 4 + 1 = 9$$

Write 9 here.

So, $236 + 117 + 151 + 451 = 955$

Add the following numbers using the drop 10 method.

1

```
    2 6 6
    2 1 3
    1 2 5
  + 2 5 6
  ─────────
```

2

```
    1 4 5
    6 5 7
    8 9 0
  + 1 1 9
  ─────────
```

3

```
    2 1 3
    4 5 6
    8 9 6
  + 2 3 3
  ─────────
```

4

```
    1 1 3
    3 4 8
    5 4 3
  + 8 7 9
  ─────────
```

5

```
    2 1 4
    4 5 5
    1 1 8
  + 3 2 1
  ─────────
```

6

```
    6 5 7
    2 1 3
    2 1 4
  + 3 4 6
  ─────────
```

7

```
    1 1 1
    3 2 4
    6 7 5
  + 1 2 5
  ─────────
```

8

```
    8 7 6
    1 2 3
    1 3 4
  + 2 1 3
  ─────────
```

9

```
    3 4 5
    6 7 8
    9 8 0
  + 6 7 8
  ─────────
```

WORD PROBLEMS

Use the drop 10 method of addition to solve the following word problems in less than a minute.

1. Sammy and his mother went to the grocer to buy some groceries. Before the grocer can calculate the final amount, help Sammy tally it! They bought: tea powder for 89; biscuit packets for 56; sugar for 72 and toothpaste for 35.

2. The radio is airing a cricket commentary and the commentator is giving out individual scores. Sum up the runs to check the final scores: Tony - 76 runs; Robby - 97 runs; Tom - 45 runs; Ali - 99 runs.

Subtracting larger numbers can be difficult at times. Use **Nikhilam** (base of the sum is 10) to make it simpler. Here are the rules:

1. Start subtracting from the left instead of the right.
2. If the digit in the upper number is less than the lower number, add the complement of the digit in the second number to the digit in the first number instead of subtracting. Whenever you do this, subtract 1 from the answer you have arrived at before this step.

Step 1

Subtract from the left first.

$3 - 1 = 2$

```
  3 7 8 2
- 1 8 9 1
  -------
  2
```

Step 2

Since 7 is greater than 8, find the Nikhilam of 8 that is 2.

$10 - 8 = 2$

```
  3 7 8 2
- 1 8 9 1
  -------
   2 9      Write 9 in the same step.
  -1        Subtract 1 from the previous answer that is 2.
```

Step 3

Again 8 is greater than 9, so take the complement of 9, that is, $10-9=1$. Add the complement 1 to 8.

Add 1 to 8 to get 9.

```
  3 7 8 2
- 1 8 9 1
  -------
   2 9 9
  -1 -1
```
Write 9. In the same step, subtract 1 from the previous answer that is 9.

Step 4

Subtract the last digits.

$2 - 1 = 1$

```
  3 7 8 2
- 1 8 9 1
  -------
   2 9 9 1      Write the answer.
  -1 -1
```

```
  3 7 8 2
- 1 8 9 1
```

Step 5

Finish off by subtracting 1 wherever required

```
  2 9 9 1
 -1 -1
```

```
  1 8 9 1
```
← Your answer.

Subtract the following numbers using Nikhilam.

1
```
  8 7 4 9
- 4 9 7 1
```

2
```
  3 6 1 9
- 1 7 8 2
```

3
```
  8 4 6 5
- 1 2 5 6
```

4
```
  5 4 3 8
- 1 5 4 6
```

5
```
  8 5 6 7
- 2 6 1 3
```

6
```
  6 8 2 7
- 1 9 1 3
```

7
```
  9 2 4 1
- 4 3 3 1
```

8
```
  6 7 6 7
- 2 8 7 3
```

13

9

```
  8 4 6 3
- 5 4 7 8
```

10

```
  7 4 3 9
- 2 7 6 8
```

11

```
  8 7 4 0
- 1 9 2 0
```

12

```
  8 6 2 8
- 2 8 1 5
```

13

```
  8 7 6 0
- 1 8 1 0
```

14

```
  7 3 2 9
- 1 7 3 2
```

15

```
  4 5 1 6
- 1 3 0 9
```

16

```
  9 5 9 1
- 2 7 0 0
```

17

```
  5 3 9 5 4
- 3 4 5 6 1
```

18

```
  8 4 6 2 1
- 6 4 7 8 1
```

19

```
  8 7 4 3 9
- 4 9 2 1 8
```

20

```
  3 2 4 6 7
- 1 4 5 6 9
```

14

SUBTRACTION WORD PROBLEMS

Use Nikhilam to solve the following word problems.

1. If there are 5674 trees in Alison's orchard and 4198 in her neighbour's, how many more trees does Alison have?

2. The cost of an air conditioner has gone up from 28971 to 34783 in summer. Calculate the difference in price.

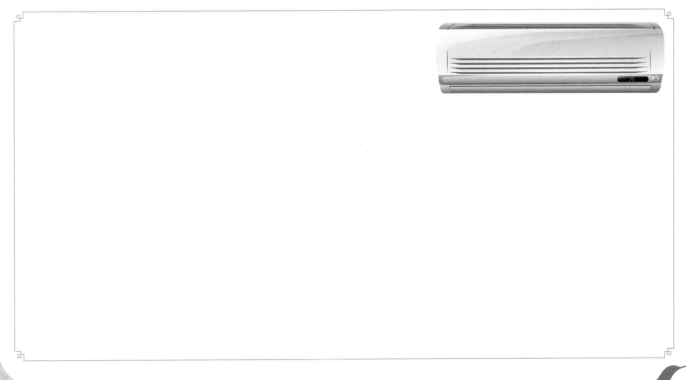

Use Nikhilam to make multiplication interesting. Just remember this mantra: "All from 9 and the last from 10" and "−" represents 10. Apply Nikhilam directly to multiply single-digit numbers that need multiplication tables of 6 and above. Instead of multiplying numbers directly, multiply their complements. Then, do a cross-addition to find the answer.

Example 1: Multiply 8 × 6

Step 1
Write the numbers as shown.

8

6

Step 2
Write the complements of both numbers.

8   − 2
6   − 4

Add the '-' sign next to them.

Step 3
Multiply the 2 complements.

8   − 2
6   − 4
_____
        8

This gives the ones digit of the answer.

Step 4
To find the tens digit of the answer, add diagonally.

8 − 2   8 − 2
6 − 4   or   6 − 4
_____   _____
  4   8   4   8

So, **8 × 6 = 48**

Example 2: Multiply 7 × 6

Step 1
Write the numbers as shown.

7

6

Step 2
Write the complements of both numbers.

7   − 3
6   − 4

Add the '-' sign next to them.

Step 3
Multiply the 2 complements.

^{1}7   − 3
6   − 4
_____
        2

This gives the ones digit of the answer.

Here, the answer is 3 × 4 = 12, so write 2 and carry over 1.

Step 4
To find the tens of the answer, add diagonally. Then, add the carried over 1.

$_1$7 − 3   7 − 3
6 − 4   or   6 − 4
_____   _____
  4   2   4   2

So, **7 × 6 = 42**

Use Nikhilam to multiply the following single-digit numbers.

1

7
× 9
_____

7 × 9 =

2

6
× 8
_____

6 × 8 =

3

8
× 9
_____

8 × 9 =

4

9
× 6
_____

9 × 6 =

5

8
× 8
_____

8 × 8 =

6

8
× 6
_____

8 × 6 =

7

6
× 6
_____

6 × 6 =

8

5
× 9
_____

5 × 9 =

9

5
× 8
_____

5 × 8 =

10

7
× 8
_____

7 × 8 =

11

9
× 9
_____

9 × 9 =

12

7
× 7
_____

7 × 7 =

MULTIPLICATION WORD PROBLEMS

Use the tricks that you have just learnt to solve the following word problems.

1. If Tom is treating 9 of his friends to ice creams and each costs Rs 8, how much does Tom have in his pocket?

2. Robbie and 8 of his friends are travelling by bus and Robbie needs to pay for all of them. Each ticket costs Rs 7. How much does Robbie have to pay?

3. Your mother needs 7 eggs to make custard and each egg costs Rs 6. How much will the eggs cost?

MULTIPLICATION: DOUBLE TO SINGLE-DIGIT NUMBERS

Nikhilam can be used while multiplying a two-digit number with a one-digit number.

Instead of multiplying the numbers directly, multiply their complements. Then, do a cross-addition to find the answer.

Example1 : Multiply **12 ✕ 7**

Step 1

Write the numbers as shown.

12
7

Step 2

Write the complements of both numbers.

12   2
7 – 3

> Put a minus sign only for the numbers less than 10.

Step 3

Multiply the 2 complements.

12   2
7 – 3
_____
– 6

> This gives the ones digit of the answer which will be in negative.

Step 4

To find the tens digit of the answer, add diagonally.

12   2
7 – 3
_____
9 – 6

Step 5

We get 9 tens and –6.

(So, subtract 6 from 90 to get the answer.)

90 – 6 = 84

Therefore, **12 ✕ 7 = 84**

Use Nikhilam to multiply the following numbers.

1

17

× 9

_____

_____

⬜ − ⬜ = ⬜

17 × 9 = ⬜

2

16

× 8

_____

_____

⬜ − ⬜ = ⬜

16 × 8 = ⬜

3

18

× 9

_____

_____

⬜ − ⬜ = ⬜

18 × 9 = ⬜

4

19

× 6 ⬜

_____

_____

⬜ − ⬜ = ⬜

19 × 6 = ⬜

5

18

× 8 ⬜

_____

_____

⬜ − ⬜ = ⬜

18 × 8 = ⬜

6

18

× 6

_____

_____

⬜ − ⬜ = ⬜

18 × 6 = ⬜

7

15
× 8

_____

15 × 8 =

8

17
× 8

_____

17 × 8 =

9

19
× 9

_____

19 × 9 =

10

17
× 7

_____

17 × 7 =

11

16
× 6

_____

16 × 6 =

12

15
× 9

_____

15 × 9 =

WORD PROBLEMS

Solve the following word problems in less than a minute.

1. 18 students require the copies of today's worksheet on Vedic Maths. Each worksheet has 5 pages and will cost Rs 9 for a copy. How much money should the class representative collect?

2. You need 7 tennis balls for tennis practice and each ball costs Rs 16. How much will you spend on the tennis balls?

3. An ice cream cone costs Rs 15 and Rita needs to buy 8 ice creams. How much will it cost Rita if you want one as well?

Use Nikhilam to multiply two two-digit numbers as well.
Follow this rule:

Number 1 (N1)	Complement (C1)
Number 2 (N2)	Complement (C2)
N1+ C2 or N2 + C1	C1 x C2

If C1 x C2 = three-digit number, keep the last two digits and carry over the digit to the hundreds place.

Example1: Multiply **75 × 90**

Step 1
Write the numbers as shown.

75

90

Step 2
Write the complements of both numbers from 100.

75   – 25

90   – 10

> Put the minus sign next to them.

Step 3
Multiply the 2 complements.

75   – 25

90   – 10
_____

50

> This gives the ones and tens digits of the answer.

25 × 10 = 250

> Since this is three-digit number, we keep 50 and carry over 2.

Step 4
To find the rest of the answer, add cross-wise.

75   – 25

90   – 10
_____

65+2 50

> Add the carry over.

Step 5
We get 67 and 50.
Write them together

So, **75 × 90 = 6750**

Use Nikhilam to multiply the following two-digit numbers.

1

87

× 80

_____

⬭ − ⬭ = ⬭

87 × 80 =

2

25

× 89

_____

⬭ − ⬭ = ⬭

25 × 89 =

3

98

× 69

_____

⬭ − ⬭ = ⬭

98 × 69 =

4

77

× 59

_____

⬭ − ⬭ = ⬭

77 × 59 =

5

94

× 65

_____

⬭ − ⬭ = ⬭

94 × 65 =

6

86

× 99

_____

⬭ − ⬭ = ⬭

86 × 99 =

7

$$66$$
$$\times\ 87$$

$$66 \times 87 =$$

8

$$59$$
$$\times\ 85$$

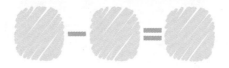

$$59 \times 85 =$$

9

$$85$$
$$\times\ 95$$

$$85 \times 95 =$$

10

$$98$$
$$\times\ 99$$

$$98 \times 99 =$$

11

$$79$$
$$\times\ 89$$

$$79 \times 89 =$$

12

$$70$$
$$\times\ 80$$

$$70 \times 80 =$$

WORD PROBLEMS

Use the trick you just learnt to solve the following word problems.

1. If each day has 24 hours, how many hours do 99 days have in all?

2. What do you get if you multiply 3 times 25 with 4 times 20?

3. If we require 87 beads to make one necklace, how many beads will be required to make 70 necklaces?

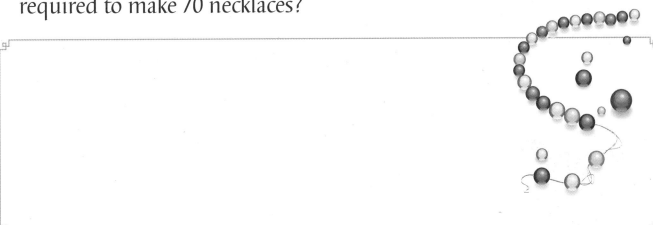

This trick makes division by 9 so simple! The quotient and the remainder are both hidden in the dividend itself. Let's find out how. Consider the number: D1D2 ÷ 9

D1 = quotient, D1 + D2 = remainder. (D1 and D2 stand for digit 1 and digit 2)

If D1 + D2 is 9 or greater than 9, the remainder is D1 + D2 −9 and increase quotient by 1.

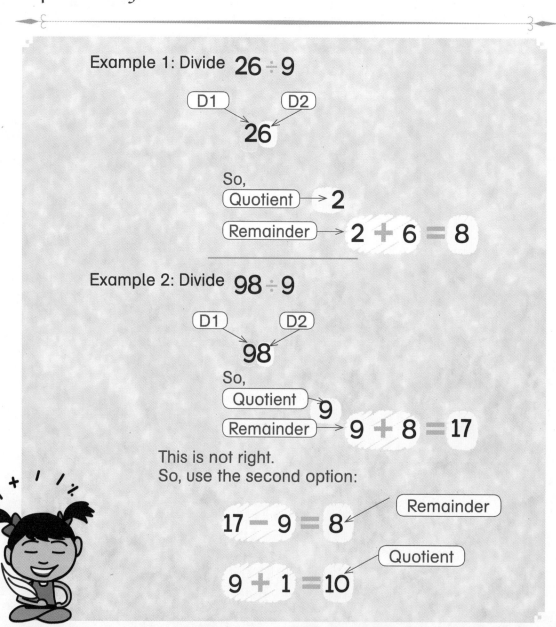

Example 1: Divide $26 \div 9$

D1   D2

26

So,

Quotient → 2

Remainder → $2 + 6 = 8$

Example 2: Divide $98 \div 9$

D1   D2

98

So,

Quotient 9

Remainder → $9 + 8 = 17$

This is not right.
So, use the second option:

$17 - 9 = 8$ ← Remainder

$9 + 1 = 10$ ← Quotient

Use Nikhilam to solve the following.

1

Q =

$32 \div 9$

R =

2

Q =

$53 \div 9$

R =

3

Q =

$62 \div 9$

R =

4

Q =

$25 \div 9$

R =

5

Q =

$72 \div 9$

R =

6

Q =

$60 \div 9$

R =

7

Q =

92 ÷ 9

R =

8

Q =

87 ÷ 9

R =

9

Q =

56 ÷ 9

R =

10

Q =

39 ÷ 9

R =

11

Q =

19 ÷ 9

R =

12

Q =

82 ÷ 9

R =

WORD PROBLEMS

Try to solve the following word problems in less than a minute.

1. 7 dozen eggs are to be divided amongst 9 houses so that all the houses get the same number of eggs. How many eggs will each house get? How many eggs will remain?

2. Anita decides to buy 1 box of 20 mangoes. She divides the mangoes among 9 of her family members, excluding her. If she wants to give equal mangoes to each member, will any be left for her?

ANSWERS

Page 3
1. 6
2. 4
3. 8
4. 7
5. 8
6. 8

Page 4
1. 9
2. 9
3. 3
4. 4
5. 4

Page 5 and 6
1. 375
2. 226
3. 879
4. 99
5. 572
6. 868
7. 8765
8. 8319
9. 3292
10. 4529

Page 8
1. 115
2. 108
3. 112
4. 116
5. 246
6. 143
7. 250
8. 233
9. 254

Page 10
1. 860
2. 1811
3. 1798
4. 1883
5. 1108
6. 1430
7. 1235
8. 1346
9. 2681

Page 11
1. 252
2. 317

Page 13 and 14
1. 3778
2. 1837
3. 7209
4. 3892
5. 5954
6. 4914
7. 4910
8. 3894
9. 2985
10. 4671
11. 6820
12. 5813
13. 6950
14. 5597
15. 3207
16. 6891
17. 19393
18. 19840
19. 38221
20. 17898

Page 15
1. 1476
2. 5812

Page 17 and 18
1. 63
2. 48
3. 72
4. 54
5. 64
6. 48
7. 36
8. 45
9. 40
10. 56
11. 81
12. 49

Page 19
1. 72
2. 56
3. 42

Page 21 and 22
1. 153
2. 128
3. 162
4. 114
5. 144
6. 108
7. 120
8. 136
9. 171
10. 119
11. 96
12. 135

Page 23
1. 162
2. 112
3. 120

Page 25 and 26
1. 6960
2. 2225
3. 6762
4. 4543
5. 6110
6. 8514
7. 5742
8. 5015
9. 8075
10. 9702
11. 7031
12. 5600

Page 27
1. 2376
2. 6000
3. 6090

Page 29 and 30
1. 3   5
2. 5   8
3. 6   8
4. 2   7
5. 8   0
6. 6   6
7. 10   2
8. 9   6
9. 6   2
10. 4   3
11. 2   1
12. 9   1

Page 31
1. Q = 9; R = 3
2. 2 mangoes for each family member and 2 for herself.